D0501459

DEC 1 3 1997

United States v. Nixon

Watergate and the President

D.J. Herda

Landmark Supreme Court Cases

ENSLOW PUBLISHERS, INC.

44 Fadem Road   P.O. Box 38

Box 699   Aldershot

Springfield, N.J. 07081   Hants GU12 6BP

U.S.A.   U.K.

THIS BOOK IS THE PROPERTY OF
THE NATIONAL CITY PUBLIC LIBRARY

Copyright ©1996 by D. J. Herda

All rights reserved.

No part of this book may be reprinted by any means
without the written permission of the publisher.

Library of Congress Cataloging–in–Publication Data

Herda, D. J., 1948-
    United States v. Nixon: Watergate and the president / D.J. Herda.
       p. cm.— (Landmark Supreme Court cases)
    Includes bibliographical references and index.
    Summary: Considers the landmark case of United States v. Nixon and the extent to
which "presidential powers" can be applied to the leader of our country.
    ISBN 0-89490-753-0
    1. United States—Trials, litigation, etc.—Juvenile literature. 2. Nixon, Richard M.
(Richard Milhous), 1913—Trials, litigation, etc.—Juvenile literature. 3. Executive
privilege (Government information)—United States—Juvenile literature. 4. Watergate
Affair, 1972–1974—Juvenile literature. [1. Nixon, Richard M. (Richard Milhous),
1913—Trials, litigation, etc. 2. Watergate Affair, 1972–1974. 3. United States—Trials,
litigation, etc.] I. Title. II. Series.
KF228.U5H47 1996
342.73'062—dc20
[347.30262]   95-31629
                                                                                CIP
                                                                                AC

Printed in the United States of America

10 9 8 7 6 5 4 3 2 1

Photo Credits: National Archives, pp. 21, 32, 43, 52, 87; Peter M. Coons, pp. 6,
12, 14, 18, 25, 37, 62, 70, 97.

Cover Illustration: AP/Wide World Photos.

Contents

1

The Beginning of the End

It was November 1972. The war in Vietnam raged on. Antiwar demonstrators marched through the streets. Richard M. Nixon was reelected to the office of president of the United States.

For a while, all went well. Then, on March 19, 1973, James McCord, a defendant in the Watergate break-in case, wrote a letter to Judge John Sirica. In it he charged that some defendants in the trial had committed perjury, lying under oath. McCord insisted that high Nixon administration officials were involved in paying the defendants to remain silent about their superiors' involvement. McCord himself had received funds from both the Committee for the Re-election of the President (CRP) and the Republican National Committee.[1] Watergate was about to split the nation in two. The

Richard Nixon discusses national affairs with his aide, H. R. Haldeman. Haldeman was later convicted on criminal charges for his part in the Watergate scandal.

Watergate affair had begun in June 1972. Several men hired by CRP had been arrested while breaking into the Democratic National Committee headquarters at the Watergate apartment-office complex in Washington, D.C. Early in 1973, they were convicted of burglary and political espionage (spying).

The United States Senate began hearings to look into claims that White House officials covered up Nixon administration involvement. Several of Nixon's top aides resigned. Nixon himself claimed executive privilege (the right of the president to withhold information) and refused to turn over tape recordings of White House conversations—recordings that might prove who was innocent and who was not.

Meanwhile, the House Judiciary Committee began an inquiry into whether or not Nixon had committed acts that were grounds for impeachment (a trial to remove him from office).

On April 30, 1974, Nixon released edited transcripts of several White House tapes. They contained conversations that would supposedly reassure the public of his innocence regarding the Watergate break-in and cover-up. Instead, the transcripts seemed to point to Nixon himself as a participant in the Watergate affair.

Was he guilty? Was he innocent? Only time—and the relentless pursuit of the truth—would tell.

2

The Early Years

The Nixons were a poor Scottish-Irish farming family. In 1731, they emigrated from Ireland to the United States. The family settled first in Delaware, then moved to Ohio, where Francis Anthony Nixon was later born. Frank, as his family and friends called him, went to school in McArthur, Ohio, through the sixth grade, when he left school to go to work. Times were difficult for immigrants in America. Jobs were hard to find, and pay was low. Frank had to do his part to contribute.

During the next few years, Frank held a number of odd jobs. Finally, he found a good job as a streetcar motorman. It was the last job he would hold in Ohio. One cold, wintry day, he came home with badly frostbitten feet. After trying unsuccessfully to get the company to enclose or heat its cars, he would no longer tolerate the cold midwestern winters. He decided to move to a warmer climate.

Frank left Ohio for California, where he took a job in the small Quaker town of Whittier, about fifteen miles east of Los Angeles. There he once again found work as a driver, this time running a trolley car.

For Frank, Whittier proved to be a much more pleasant environment than Ohio, and not only because of the weather. It became a very special place for him— the place where he first fell in love. In February 1908, Frank met Hannah Milhous at a Quaker meetinghouse.

Hannah was one of nine children born to the Milhous family. Her ancestors had lived in Germany, England, and Ireland. The Milhouses were Quakers who had sought freedom to practice their religion without interference from their neighbors or government.

Religious freedom was rare in Europe in the 1700s, and many people came to America, where stories of religious freedom and tolerance were more common. In 1729, the Milhouses moved to the United States. They settled in Pennsylvania before moving to Butlerville, Indiana, where Hannah was later born. In 1897, they moved to Whittier.

Four months after Hannah met Frank, the two were married. Frank, who had been raised a Methodist, became a Quaker. The young couple had Harold, the first of their five sons, in 1909. Three years later, Frank bought a parcel of land in Yorba Linda, a small farming village in Orange County, California. He built a house and moved his family there in 1912. He planted lemon trees and hoped to earn a living from the grove.

Their second son, Richard Milhous Nixon, was born in that house on January 9, 1913. Named after King Richard the Lion-Hearted of England, he was one of four sons to be named after English kings. Two of Richard's four brothers, Francis Donald and Arthur, were also born in Yorba Linda.

Although Yorba Linda eventually grew into a beautiful and prosperous community, the Nixons did not do well as citrus farmers. After nearly a decade of struggling to make a living from the lemon groves, Frank quit farming and moved back to Whittier. Edward, the last of the Nixon children, was born there in 1930.

Faced once again with the question of how to earn a living, Frank opened a combination gas station and grocery store. His in-laws helped him get started by loaning him money. Three years later, he bought an old Quaker meetinghouse and had it moved next to the station. The house served as a general store. As the Nixon boys grew up, they helped run the family business. This was where young Richard first learned how to deal with people. "I sold gas and delivered groceries and met a lot of people," Nixon later recalled. "I think this was invaluable as a start on a public career."[1]

Richard's mother was a devoted Quaker, a patient parent, and a hard worker. His father was a strict and serious man who early in life had developed a keen interest in politics. He also founded a neighborhood debating club whose members met at the market to discuss the most popular issues of the day—from religious freedom and economics to life in Europe and the benefits of immigrating to America.

Young Richard was influenced by the people who met at the club. While most boys his age were out playing baseball or riding bicycles, Richard was reading the newspapers and dreaming of the day when he, too, would take part in the debates.

Richard's father, who proved to be a strong influence on his son's life, helped him prepare for his first grammar-school debate. The subject was the advantages of renting a house rather than buying one. Richard's debating teacher, Norma Vincent, was impressed with her student. "He was so good it kind of disturbed me. He had this ability to kind of slide around an argument, instead of meeting it head on, and he could take any side of a debate."[2]

Life for the Nixon family centered around their religion. They attended services at the Quaker meetinghouse three

Richard Nixon first learned how to deal with people at his parents' general store in Whittier, California.

times each Sunday and once on Wednesdays. Richard played the organ there. One of the highlights of the year for the Nixon children was the family's Christmas get-together, which they celebrated at their grandmother Milhous's home in Whittier.

Life for the Nixons was not without pain. Arthur, the second youngest of the five Nixon boys, died unexpectedly at the age of seven. Harold contracted tuberculosis when Richard was still in high school. Hannah took him to Arizona for his health, but he died there in 1933.

Despite the tragedies, the family kept up their faith and their belief in hard work. Richard and Francis Donald toiled at keeping house and at helping to run the family business while their mother was in Arizona. Richard's job was to care for the fruits and vegetables. Each morning at 4:00 A.M., he drove the family truck twelve miles to the produce market in Los Angeles, purchased a load of fruit and vegetables, and returned to the store. Then he washed the produce and arranged it on the counter—all before school started for the day.

Each afternoon, Richard worked several more hours in the store, then studied in his room, often until midnight. His self-discipline and desire to succeed earned him top grades and a reputation as the high school's leading scholar.

Young Richard Nixon was known as a good scholar and an excellent debater.

When Richard graduated at the age of seventeen, he had hopes of attending Harvard University; but his parents still needed his help at the store. He applied for a scholarship to nearby Whittier College. It was not Harvard, but it was a good school with a solid reputation, and Richard Milhous Nixon was determined to make the best of his life there.

3

Attorney Richard M. Nixon

At the age of seventeen, Richard Nixon entered Whittier College—a small, independent Quaker college that his mother had attended. In his first year there, he proved himself a champion debater and was elected president of his class. His achievements were due not to his popularity but rather to his debating skills. He had run for president and won because of his well-run political organization and hard work.

Following his election—true to his word—he went to campus officials and convinced them that it would be better to hold dances at the college than to have Whittier's students travel to Los Angeles for their entertainment.

As a sophomore, Nixon represented Whittier in more than fifty school debates. He won most of them. By the time he entered his senior year, he was voted president of the entire student body.

To improve his debating skills, Nixon joined the drama class, where he continued developing his ability to speak publicly. Although he was a "loner," shy and awkward in small groups, he was more comfortable when addressing a large crowd.[1]

Nixon majored in history, a subject at which he did particularly well. Science and mathematics were much tougher for him, but with his hard work and long hours of study, he managed to finish second in his graduating class in 1934.

Nixon's goal in life was to become a lawyer. His brother's tuberculosis had deflated the family's savings, so he would need financial help to enter law school. That help came in the form of a scholarship to the newly established Duke University Law School in Durham, North Carolina. He graduated third in his class.

Following graduation, Nixon applied for a position at several New York law firms. He was turned down by them all. Then he applied for a job working for the Federal Bureau of Investigation (FBI), headed by J. Edgar Hoover, but he did not get the job. He then applied for a job with the law firm of Wingert and

Not only was Richard Nixon voted the president of the student body in college, he graduated second in his class—a true politician was born.

Bewley in Whittier. Young Nixon was accepted. He was paid $250 a month, which was a good salary at the time. Only a week after being admitted to the California Bar in 1937, he had his first case as a trial lawyer, representing a Los Angeles woman who was attempting to recover money owed to her. During the case, Nixon was accused by the judge of unethical behavior and was threatened with disbarment. His law firm was also sued by their client for mishandling the case. Bewley finally settled the case.

It was not a good start for Nixon's professional life, but he was a man of determination. When a business opportunity arose, along with a chance to make more money, he took it. Nixon helped organize a company called Citra-Frost, which planned to market frozen orange juice in plastic bags. The plan failed, however, and after eighteen months of hard work, the new company went out of business.

Meanwhile, Nixon's legal career had taken a turn for the better. He soon proved to be a far more capable attorney than his first case had indicated. Within a short time, Thomas Bewley made him a partner in the firm.

In 1938, five years after Bewley had become the Whittier city attorney, Bewley named his young partner to the position of assistant city attorney. For entertainment, Nixon joined the Whittier Little Theater Group, where he met Pat Ryan.

Thelma Catherine Patricia "Pat" Ryan was a high-school teacher in Whittier. She was born on March 16, 1912, in Ely, Nevada.

When she was only a year old, Pat's family moved to a ten-acre truck farm in California, where Pat was raised. Then tragedy struck. Her mother died of cancer when Pat was only thirteen, and her father died four years later.

In 1931, after attending Fullerton Junior College for one year, Pat drove an elderly couple to New York City. While there, she took a job working in a New York hospital. She worked first as a secretary, then as an X-ray technician. With the money she managed to save, she returned to the West Coast and entered the University of Southern California (USC). She earned college funds by working in a department store and as an extra in Hollywood, where she acted in several small movies. She graduated in 1937 and began teaching in Whittier.

While acting in the Whittier Little Theater Group, Pat Ryan met Richard Nixon. On June 21, 1940, two years after their first meeting, they were married. She was twenty-eight; he was a year younger.

On December 7, 1941, following the Japanese bombing of Pearl Harbor, Hawaii, the United States entered World War II. Nixon went to work in Washington, D.C. Two months later, he applied to the Navy for a commission as an officer. In September 1942,

Nixon met the love of his life at the Whittier Little Theatre Group—Thelma Catherine Patricia "Pat" Ryan, a high-school teacher.

he was made a lieutenant junior grade and was stationed in the South Pacific.

During much of the war, Nixon served as an operations officer with the South Pacific Combat Air Transport Command. He rose to the rank of lieutenant commander while overseeing the construction of air landing strips on jungle islands.[2]

After his tour of duty in the South Pacific, Nixon returned to the United States, where he was assigned to work on Navy contracts until his discharge papers came through. He was working in Baltimore, Maryland, when some friends called and told him of an advertisement that had been placed in the Whittier newspapers:

> WANTED: Congressman candidate with no previous political experience to defeat a man who has represented the district in the House [of Representatives] for 10 years. Any young man resident of district, preferably a veteran, fair education, may apply for the job.[3]

Nixon had never seriously considered entering politics, but he'd always been interested in political affairs. Suddenly, he became very interested in running for Congress.[4] After he was recommended to the committee of Republican leaders who had placed the ad, Nixon was offered the position. He would run for the House of Representatives, and the Republican party would support him—although some Republican committee members were still not convinced that he was the best man for the job. As one leader said, "He was the best of a bad lot."[5]

Nonetheless, in December 1945, Nixon accepted the candidacy. He opened his campaign the following February with the promise that he would "wage a fighting, rocking, socking campaign."[6]

Nixon would run against Jerry Voorhis, a Democrat who had represented the Twelfth District since 1936. Earlier in his life, Voorhis had been a Socialist, which many Americans at the time viewed to be the same as a Communist. As the years passed, Voorhis's views mellowed. He even spoke out against the Communist party on numerous occasions.

Nixon came up with a stroke of political genius. He geared his campaign to America's postwar anticommunist voters. He made his first political appearances dressed in a crisp, clean, blue navy uniform. He attacked Voorhis as being soft on communism and a "friend of the communists."[7] To further make his point, throughout the campaign Nixon associated Voorhis with a Communist-dominated Political Action Committee (PAC), which itself was divided over support for Voorhis. The California branch of the PAC opposed Voorhis, whom it knew to be a member of the House Un-American Activities Committee (which would become the House Committee on Un-American Activities) and a dedicated anticommunist. The national PAC organization, however, actually had endorsed Voorhis, which lent credibility to Nixon's attacks. Nixon referred to Voorhis and his supporters as "the PAC candidate and his Communist friends." "A vote for Nixon is a vote against the Communist–dominated PAC" was Nixon's campaign slogan.[8]

The campaign was tightly fought, with neither candidate ahead. Then, on February 21, 1946, Nixon's wife gave birth to the couple's first daughter, Tricia. (Their second daughter, Julie, would be born July 5, 1948.) Voorhis had a personal policy of sending pamphlets on infant care to all new parents in his district, so he sent one to the Nixons. On it he wrote, "Congratulations. I look forward to meeting you soon in public."[9]

Appearing in public shortly after his daughter's birth, Nixon read Voorhis's message aloud, insisting that Voorhis obviously had meant to commit himself to a series of public debates. This, of course, was right up Nixon's alley. Voorhis, not wanting to appear guilty of going back on his word, reluctantly agreed.[10]

Nixon's debating skills overwhelmed Voorhis, who had not spoken much in public. During each of the five debates, which began in September, Nixon made sure to refer to Voorhis's "un-American elements."[11]

When election day finally arrived, Nixon rode to

Nixon was elected to his first term in Congress by representing himself as an anticommunist. Later, as president, he made a journey to the Soviet Union to discuss political matters with Leonid I. Brezhnev. During their meeting, they agreed to limit the production of nuclear weapons.

victory as part of a nationwide trend favoring Republican candidates. His 65,586 votes far outnumbered his opponent's. Even more importantly, Nixon had discovered a critical political tactic—one that he would use in campaigns for decades to come. Nixon had represented himself as a strict anticommunist. His opponent had not. That alone, it appeared, was enough to spell the difference between victory and defeat.

During his first term in the Eightieth Congress, Nixon was assigned to the House Committee on Un-American Activities, whose purpose was to investigate anti-American plots and activities.

He was quickly gaining notoriety as the most eager anticommunist legislator in the House. In an era when many Americans feared a Communist behind every door, Richard M. Nixon represented freedom, integrity, and the American way of life.

4

From Senator to Vice President

The House Committee on Un-American Activities continued to grow in stature and in strength until it was one of the most widely-known and greatly-feared committees in Congress. The years following the end of World War II saw a division in world politics that loosely translated into "we" and "they." We—Americans—were the good guys, the defenders of freedom, the anticommunists. They—the Communists and Socialists—were the bad guys, the tyrants.

Soviet Russia, with its lack of free elections and its authoritarian rule, led the Communist world. The United States, with its personal freedoms and democratic rule, led the free world. Between the two countries and their allies fell an invisible "iron curtain" that separated the two ways of life.

Nixon's tireless devotion to the House Committee on Un-American Activities brought him more publicity, more power, and more support daily. Still, there was something missing.

In August 1948, Nixon heard the testimony of Whittaker Chambers, a self-confessed former-Communist espionage agent. Chambers named Alger Hiss, who had been a United States State Department official during the administration of President Franklin D. Roosevelt, as a Communist sympathizer. This is exactly what Nixon and the House Committee on Un-American Activities had been waiting for.

At first, the House committee and Nixon pursued the case in the privacy of closed-door sessions. Nixon brought Chambers and Hiss together, as in a trial. Chambers showed the committee what he claimed was proof that Hiss had passed State Department secrets to him—a violation of United States espionage laws. Chambers went so far as to produce several rolls of microfilm that he had hidden in a pumpkin on his farm near Westminster, Maryland—microfilm he claimed Hiss had given him. Eventually, Nixon leaked the sworn testimony of Chambers to a curious American public.

Only Nixon, it appeared, was convinced of Hiss's Communist ties. In the months that followed the increasingly publicized hearings, however, the American public slowly began to come around to Richard Nixon's way of thinking.

Finally, on December 15, 1948, Hiss was indicted (accused of committing a crime) by a New York federal grand jury. The charge was perjury. More than two years later, after two long, rambling trials, Hiss was convicted and sentenced to five years in prison. Alger Hiss became a national disgrace. Richard Nixon was a hero.

While the Hiss case was still in the courts, Nixon came up for reelection to his congressional seat in Whittier. He was so popular that he was nominated in both the Republican and the Democratic primaries. He won reelection easily.

By 1950, with his popularity among the American public at an all-time high, Nixon announced his candidacy for the United States Senate.[1] Running against him was popular California congresswoman Helen Gahagan Douglas, a liberal Democrat and a former Hollywood actress.

Nixon, who by now had learned the value of running a campaign based on anticommunism, referred to his opponent as "the Pink Lady."[2] (From the 1950s to the 1970s, the word *pink* was often used to describe someone thought to be a Communist.) He accused her of being a Communist sympathizer and of having Communist ties in government. "You, and you can't deny it," he wrote to Douglas in one of his most harsh pieces of campaign literature, "have earned the praise of communist and pro-communist newspapers for opposing the very things Nixon has stood for."[3]

Nixon went on to publish *The Pink Sheet*, a newsletter on pink paper that contained campaign notes and attacks on Douglas, and which his campaign committee distributed to more than half a million California voters. In it, he accused Douglas of voting the same way as a "notorious communist-line congressman" from New York on 354 separate occasions.[4] What Nixon failed to point out was that Douglas had opposed that very same congressman on hundreds of other issues and that Nixon himself had voted with the congressman more than one hundred times. Because of these campaign techniques, which many politicians and members of the press viewed as underhanded and unfair, Nixon soon earned the nickname Tricky Dick.[5]

Nixon won a landslide victory over Douglas. Now it seemed that nothing could stop him. The youngest member of the United States Senate at age thirty-eight, Richard Nixon was not about to let up on his anticommunist campaigns.

As a senator, Nixon spent a good deal of time supporting General Douglas MacArthur in his attempt to secure a victory for the United States and its allies in Korea. He also championed various congressional plans of support for Generalissimo Chiang Kai-shek (jyahng ky SHEHK), who was fighting for control of his native China from the Communists, who were led by Mao Tse-tung (mow zen dawng). At home, Nixon worked his way onto Senator Joe McCarthy's committee to expose Communists in Hollywood and in the arts.

While all this was going on, Nixon kept a watchful eye on the developing battle for the 1952 Republican presidential nomination. One group of Republicans backed General Dwight D. Eisenhower for the nomination. Another pushed for Senator Robert Taft. As it turned out, Eisenhower was nominated, and Nixon, who had worked hard on Eisenhower's behalf, was rewarded with the nomination for vice president. Not everyone in the party was pleased with the vice presidential selection. As one Republican commented, "We took Dick Nixon not because he was right wing [conservative] or left wing [liberal]—but because he came from California and we were tired."[6]

Despite the lack of support, Nixon worked hard during the presidential campaign. At every stop, he pounded away at three major issues—the Korean War,

Pat Nixon stood by her husband throughout his years as a public figure—for better or for worse.

the Democratic party's soft spot for communism, and corruption among the Democrats. This last attack very nearly backfired, and could have cost the Republicans the election, when Nixon himself was charged with taking illegal campaign contributions.

On September 18, the headlines in the *New York Post* read, "Secret Nixon Fund." The follow-up story claimed that sixty-six wealthy Californians had secretly contributed a total of more than $18,000 for Nixon's personal use while he was in the Senate. Voters across the country were shocked. Party members were horrified.[7] As pressure mounted for Nixon to withdraw from the election, he decided to go on national television to denounce the reports. He invited the press to examine his finances. He insisted that none of his supporters had ever received political favors in return for their contributions. In his famous "Checkers" speech, he firmly maintained his innocence.

He did, however, admit to having taken one thing:

> A man down in Texas heard Pat on the radio mention the fact that our two youngsters would like to have a dog and, believe it or not, the day before we left on this campaign trip we got a message from Union Station in Baltimore, saying they had a package for us. We went down to get it. You know what it was? It was a little cocker spaniel dog, in a crate that had been sent all the way from Texas—black and white, spotted, and our little girl Tricia, the six-year-old, named it Checkers. And you know, the kids, like all kids, loved the dog, and

I just want to say this, right now, that regardless of what
they say about it, we are going to keep it.[8]

The speech was a political triumph. Thousands of
cards, letters, and telegrams flooded Republican national
headquarters, the great majority in support of Nixon.
Eisenhower asked Nixon to come to Wheeling, West
Virginia, where he was campaigning. The future
president put aside any doubts that he may have had and,
in a public display of unity, told Nixon, "Dick, you're
my boy."[9]

Eisenhower's public comment did little to convince
the Democrats that everything was fine in the Republican
camp. Adlai Stevenson, the Democratic nominee for
president and a longtime participant in national politics,
was quick to pick up on the Nixon charges. If the
Republicans "will stop telling lies about us," Stevenson
said, "we will stop telling the truth about them."[10]

In the end, Nixon's defense against the charges won
out. On November 4, 1952, the Republicans won a
landslide victory. Stevenson, commenting on the results
after the election, said he felt the way Abraham Lincoln
had felt after losing an election—like a little boy who
stubbed his toe in the dark. "He was too old to cry, but it
hurt too much to laugh."[11]

The 1952 victory was the greatest triumph of Nixon's
young political life. His transformation from an obscure

congressman out of California, to vice president of the United States in only six years was remarkable.

Personality conflicts soon arose between Eisenhower and Nixon, however. Eisenhower was a former military-man, a straight-shooting administrator with a general dislike for politics and politicians. Nixon, on the other hand, was a shrewd and crafty politician. He knew how to control voters, win elections, and pressure party members into his way of thinking.

While Eisenhower had to tolerate Nixon's presence as vice president for the next four years, he did not have to add to Nixon's already glowing image. Eisenhower avoided giving Nixon any meaningful tasks to complete as vice president. When the 1956 campaign for reelection rolled around, Eisenhower tried his best to get Nixon to withdraw from the national ticket by offering him a cabinet post. But Nixon declined.[12]

Republican party officials, anxious to avoid any appearance of disunity or disharmony within their ranks, persuaded Eisenhower to accept Nixon as his running mate once again. Eisenhower reluctantly agreed, and the Eisenhower-Nixon team was swept into office for a second term.

Throughout his second four-year term, Eisenhower continued to distance himself from Nixon. He gave his vice president little to do of importance and made every attempt to keep him away from the White House. He sent him on nine different trips to sixty-one countries on almost every continent in the world.

Once, in 1960, a reporter asked Eisenhower what major decisions the vice president had participated in during his administration. Eisenhower thought about the question for a few moments and then casually replied, "If you give me a week, I might think of one."[13]

Nixon, on the other hand, was his party's front-running candidate for president in 1960. (Eisenhower would be forced to step down because of a two-term limit recently placed on presidents by the addition of the Twenty-Second Amendment to the United States Constitution.) As vice president, Nixon had the advantage of tremendous national publicity from his travels. In 1959, he devised a plan to place his name before every voting American. At the same time, he could gain an advantage over his political adversary in the upcoming election, a young Massachusetts senator by the name of John Fitzgerald Kennedy.

The State Department decided to send Nixon to the Soviet Union, reminding Nixon that his appearance there would be purely ceremonial. When Nixon arrived for his meeting with Premier Nikita Khrushchev (KROOSH chehf), he could not resist debating the Soviet leader over which form of government was better—United States

Years before Richard Nixon was elected president in 1968, he was the vice president of the Eisenhower administration.

democracy or Soviet communism. The cameras closely followed the continuing debate and sent home film of Nixon firmly defending the American way of life. Film clips showed the vice president shaking his finger at Khrushchev and criticizing the Soviet leader for his country's Communist ways. When Nixon returned to the United States, his popularity in America was higher than ever.

Nixon approached the upcoming 1960 presidential election as the best-known political name in America. He was running against a relative unknown. Nixon's hopes soared even further when Kennedy challenged him to a series of nationally televised debates. He was convinced that he would humiliate the young senator before millions of voters. "Start in low key and work to a crescendo [peak] in the last two weeks," he told his campaign staffers.[14]

Eisenhower and other Republicans warned Nixon not to accept the challenge. He didn't need the debates. He was, after all, the vice president, and far better known than Kennedy.

Nixon ignored the advice. He also ignored advice to rest before the first debate. Instead, he continued his whirlwind campaign tour until the very last minute.

On the day of the first Great Debate, as the press labeled the event, the vice president banged his knee against the door of his car. The pain from the injury showed clearly on his face. A record 80 million Americans, who knew nothing of the accident, saw a televised Nixon who looked unshaved, tired, and grumpy. Kennedy, by contrast, appeared tanned, fresh, and alert.

The debate was the first of a long series of political mistakes that Nixon would make over the coming years. To him, it was merely a minor setback on his way to the White House. But time, and a few thousand votes, would prove him wrong.

5

Falling from Grace

To run as vice president with Nixon in the 1960 presidential election, the Republicans chose Henry Cabot Lodge, Jr., a former senator of Massachusetts and ambassador to the United Nations for eight years. Kennedy, on the other hand, chose as his running mate a longtime senator from Texas, Lyndon B. Johnson.

To win his party's primary nomination at the Democratic National Convention in Los Angeles, Kennedy had beaten a popular senator from Minnesota, Hubert H. Humphrey. In his acceptance speech, Kennedy spoke enthusiastically of a "new frontier." He wanted to get the country moving once again and called for "a new generation of leadership—new men to cope with new problems and new opportunities."[1]

Nixon, like Kennedy, promised to move America

forward. Unlike Kennedy, who proposed new government programs to deal with old problems, Nixon emphasized the value of relying on private enterprise and reduced government spending.

Nixon also promised to visit all fifty states during his campaign. He got off to a slow start, however, because of an infection in his recently reinjured knee. His advisers suggested that he retract his promise, but Nixon refused. He was anxious to make up for lost time and quickly set out on a grueling cross-country campaign trail.

Whenever possible, Nixon referred to Kennedy's youth and inexperience in national affairs. He pointed out that he, on the other hand, had traveled widely while in the Eisenhower administration—even going to the Soviet Union to debate the leader of the Communist world.

Kennedy was not intimidated by Nixon's attacks. He told the voters that he—like Nixon—had entered Congress in 1946 and had served his country for fourteen years. Kennedy admitted that the vice president was indeed more experienced—"experienced in policies of retreat, defeat, and weakness" that were causing a decline in America's image throughout the world.[2]

Following the first debate between the two presidential candidates, national polls showed that most Americans felt Kennedy had come off looking better than Nixon.[3] The senator had appeared calm, poised, and self-assured, while Nixon (suffering from the knee injury and showing signs of a recent bout with the flu) had looked tired, angry, and defensive.

The results concerned Nixon. Prior to the second debate, he gained some weight, used better makeup to hide his beard stubble, and rested.

Kennedy, too, was hard at work preparing for the next debate. He studied the issues Nixon was likely to raise, especially those concerning foreign affairs. He memorized facts and statistics that might prove useful. He even inserted a few jokes and personal stories that he felt might appeal to his viewing audience. As a result, Nixon once again came off second best, while Kennedy seemed to be more knowledgeable and sure of himself.

On October 19, two days before the last of the four debates, Kennedy received word that the Reverend Martin Luther King, Jr., the popular civil rights activist, had been arrested with fifty-two other African-Americans while demonstrating against segregation in Atlanta, Georgia. King was sentenced to four months in jail. Kennedy immediately telephoned his brother, Robert, who contacted the judge in the case. Robert arranged to pay King's bail, and the civil rights leader was released.

Meanwhile, Nixon, who had also heard of the arrest, decided that it would not look good to the nation for the vice president to get involved with a controversial figure

Though Nixon prided himself on being an excellent public speaker, his poor showing in televised debates against John F. Kennedy led to his loss in the 1960 presidential election.

like King. As a result, King's father, Martin Luther King, Sr., who was a Protestant minister and had been a Republican, changed his mind about voting for Nixon and announced to the press that he had decided to back Kennedy. "I've got a suitcase of votes [from his followers], and I'm going to take them to Mr. Kennedy and dump them in his lap," the elder King said.[4]

Through his actions, Kennedy had taken a giant step forward in securing the African-American vote. Nixon, through his inaction, had miscalculated the campaign.

By mid-October, the race for president had become too close to call. George Gallup, whose political polls are among the most accurate in the nation, refused to predict the outcome.

On election day, November 8, Kennedy surged ahead to take a sizeable lead over Nixon; but as day turned to night, the young senator's lead slowly shrank. The race was so close that no one was able to determine who had won for two days. Finally, the results were in. The race had provided the largest voter turnout in United States history—more than 68 million Americans had cast their votes. The results: Kennedy won by fewer than one hundred twenty thousand votes. Nixon got 49.55 percent of the total votes cast; Kennedy, 49.71 percent. Senator Harry Byrd and several other candidates received the rest of the votes. In terms of states won, Nixon had

26 for a total of 219 electoral votes. Kennedy carried only 22 states but won 303 electoral votes.

After the election, some Nixon supporters blamed the defeat on voter fraud, especially in Texas and Illinois, two solidly Democratic states. Others pinned the loss on Nixon's poor showing in the debates. Still others blamed the defeat on Eisenhower's unwillingness to campaign for his former vice president.

In reality, Kennedy's victory was due to a number of factors. He was young, handsome, witty, and intelligent. He pulled a great deal of support from the nation's large Roman-Catholic population. He had sought and captured the African-American vote. The fact that the Democrats had won the last three congressional elections and held thirty-four governorships also helped Kennedy. The Republicans, on the other hand, failed to secure the support of organized labor, and their social welfare programs were no match for those of the Democrats.

On January 20, 1961, John Fitzgerald Kennedy became the youngest man ever—and the first Roman Catholic—to hold the office of president. Richard M. Nixon, down but not out, returned to his home in California to think about his political future.

6

On the Road to the White House

Although Nixon's political future was clouded, his choices were clear. He could retire from politics and return to practicing law until he had another chance to run for the office of president in four years. Or he could run for another important political position, which at least would keep his name before the American public.

After several months of practicing law in New York, Nixon decided to seek the office of governor of California. His reasoning was simple. His loss to Kennedy in the 1960 presidential campaign was the first political defeat of his life, and it had left a bad taste in his mouth. He did not like being labeled a loser, and he would do whatever it took to change that image.[1]

Meanwhile, in 1962, California governor Edmund G. "Pat" Brown announced his decision to run for another term. It was the perfect opportunity for Nixon to unseat the Democrat. Nixon had a strong political following in his home state. When New York governor Nelson Rockefeller proposed that Nixon run for the office, Nixon agreed.[2]

So in 1962, Nixon launched a statewide campaign in which he accused Brown of being dangerously left-wing. It was a campaign trick that had worked for him in the past.

Nixon's campaign, though, went poorly from the beginning. One of the biggest reasons was news in the press of a secret $200,000 loan from billionaire Howard Hughes to Nixon's brother, Donald. Wherever he went, the press wanted to know about the loan. Nixon had no good answer.

Another reason for Nixon's poor showing was the idea that he was running for the governorship of California merely as a stepping-stone to the presidency in 1964. Nixon himself added to the voters' fears when he slipped up during an interview and referred to himself as a candidate for "governor of the U.S."[3]

Nixon spent election day, November 6, 1962, glued to the television set, watching the statewide voter returns. They did not look good. Brown jumped out to an early lead and continued to build on it until he had pulled ahead by some three hundred fifty thousand votes. When it was obvious that he had lost, Nixon went to the convention hall to deliver his concession speech. He appeared before the cameras, unshaved and still wearing the suit he had put on early that morning.

Finally he began his speech, which quickly turned into an attack on the press in what would become one of the best-known political speeches of all time:

> Now that all the members of the press are so delighted that I have lost . . . I believe Governor Brown has a heart, even though he believes that I do not . . . I did not win. I have no hard feelings against anybody, against any opponent and least of all the people of California . . . And as I leave the press, all I can say is this: For sixteen years, ever since the [Alger] Hiss case, you've had a lot of fun—a lot of fun—that you've had an opportunity to attack me . . . Just think about how much you're going to be missing. You won't have Nixon to kick around anymore, because, gentlemen, this is my last press conference.[4]

Newspapers around the country carried the highlights of the speech. It was the end, they predicted, of Richard M. Nixon's political career, and indeed it seemed to be.

For the next two years, Nixon went back to practicing law with a prosperous Wall Street law firm, which became Nixon, Mudge, Rose, Guthrie, and Alexander. His salary was $200,000 a year, which many people thought was enough to keep him in private practice for the rest of his life. His name was all but forgotten within political circles.

In 1964, however, Nixon reemerged. This time, he hit the campaign trail for Republican presidential candidate Barry M. Goldwater—but to no avail. Goldwater lost the election to Lyndon B. Johnson who pulled off a landslide victory.

Two years later, in 1966, Nixon found himself once again in politics. He traveled thirty thousand miles, visiting thirty-five states in support of eighty-seven Republican congressional candidates. Largely as a result of his efforts, the Republicans gained forty-seven House seats, eight governorships, and three seats in the Senate. Slowly but surely, the Republicans put together a strong, unified party to make a run at the presidency in the 1968 election.[5]

Between 1964 and 1968, Nixon's efforts on behalf of the Republican party helped raise more than $5 million for campaign expenses. He announced for the second time in his career that he intended to run for the office of president of the United States.

Nixon campaigned hard—the only way he knew how. He traveled throughout the country in search of the primary election victories he would need to capture the Republican party's presidential nomination. Nixon was beginning to shed his image as a political loser. He won primary elections in New Hampshire, Wisconsin,

Indiana, Nebraska, Oregon, Pennsylvania, New Jersey, and South Dakota.

Throughout the campaign, Nixon attacked the failures of the administration of Lyndon B. Johnson, who had become president when Kennedy was assassinated in 1963. Nixon deplored the growing national crime rate, attacked the high cost of Democratic welfare programs, and denounced the country's rising inflation rate.

By the time the Republican National Convention met in Miami Beach, Florida, Nixon's only stumbling block to the presidential nomination was Nelson A. Rockefeller, the outspoken Republican governor of New York. But Rockefeller finally lost to Nixon, who went on to win a sweeping first-ballot victory, gathering nearly seven hundred votes. Rockefeller pulled only 277.

As his running mate, Nixon selected Maryland governor Spiro T. Agnew, who was largely unknown outside his own state. A conservative southern candidate could cost Nixon big-city and liberal votes that he badly needed in the North. Similarly, a liberal northern Republican would cost him conservative votes in the South, a region that had backed Nixon solidly at the convention. Agnew was a compromise choice acceptable to both North and South. Besides, Nixon reasoned, Agnew's relative obscurity in national politics would make it difficult for the press to criticize his running mate.

Meanwhile, the Democratic party was also hard at work preparing for the coming 1968 election. Johnson was clearly the front-runner to receive the Democratic party's nomination—at least until the thunder erupted. In a nationally televised speech on March 31, 1967, Johnson announced that he would not run for a second term as president. "I shall not seek and I will not accept the nomination of my party for another term," he said.[6]

Scurrying around for a candidate to replace Johnson, Democratic party leaders convinced the vice president, Hubert H. Humphrey, to enter the race.

At the 1968 Democratic National Convention in Chicago, Humphrey won his party's presidential nomination. As his running mate, he chose Maine senator Edmund Muskie, who also was quickly approved.

The Democratic convention suddenly hit a snag. Party doves, those in favor of immediate withdrawal from the conflict in Vietnam, demanded that Humphrey adopt a policy calling for the complete withdrawal of all United States troops from Vietnam and an immediate end to the fighting. The hawks, who believed America should settle for nothing less than a complete military victory, wanted a continuation of the policy begun by Johnson. They promoted international peace talks and a conditional end to United States bombing, provided North Vietnam responded in kind.

Richard Nixon's run for the presidency in 1968 was successful mainly because the opposing Democrats did not show a united front. Not only did Nixon have the full support of his party, his family stood behind him 100 percent.

Outside the convention center, thousands of antiwar demonstrators, led by the National Mobilization Committee to End the War in Vietnam, demonstrated against White House war policies. Chicago Mayor Richard J. Daley—a powerful leader in national Democratic politics—was determined not to let the demonstrators gain the upper hand. "No one," he insisted, "is going to take over the streets."[7]

Daley ordered the city's nearly twelve thousand police officers into round-the-clock duty. He called in thousands of Illinois National Guard troops for reinforcement. Within hours, the city looked like a war zone.

Daley had misjudged the dedication of the demonstrators to the peace movement. At a rally held in Grant Park, police fired tear gas into the crowd, scattering thousands of people, who merely regrouped and continued their demonstration elsewhere. In Lincoln Park, police attacked demonstrators with nightsticks and drawn guns.

As televised news reports of the demonstrators spread across the nation, delegates to the Democratic convention were shocked. Connecticut senator Abraham Ribicoff shouted from the podium, "Gestapo tactics in the streets of Chicago!" One delegate from Wisconsin shouted, "Thousands of young people are being beaten on the streets of Chicago! I move this convention be adjourned for two weeks and moved to another city."[8]

The convention was not adjourned, but the Democratic party's problems stole some of the limelight from Humphrey's nomination. Furthermore, the images of the convention-day riots would haunt the party throughout the campaign.

Meanwhile, Nixon was running for office on a platform that pledged to bring peace, law, and order back to America. He appealed to millions of Americans fed up with both the war and the antiwar protests. He had everything that Humphrey lacked, including a united party, a smooth-running campaign, and plenty of money to run his campaign. In public, he appeared informed and confident. As he traveled the country, he promised that, if elected, he would end the war honorably, although he never revealed how he planned to do this.

While Nixon was pulling ahead of Humphrey in the polls, he faced a growing problem in the form of an independent candidate who also had decided to run for president. George Wallace was the former governor of Alabama. When he failed to get the Democratic party's nomination for president, he turned to the American Independent party, which agreed to support his presidential bid. Although Wallace never thought he could win the election, he hoped to obtain at least enough votes to be able to persuade the winning party to adopt some of his policies, especially those against integration and in favor of law and order.

But Wallace's campaign was too little and too late to affect the outcome of the election. On November 5, 1968, more than 73 million voters went to the polls to cast their ballots. The results gave Richard Nixon a victory of 510,315 votes over Humphrey.

In his victory speech, Nixon stressed his goal of uniting all Americans: "This will be an open administration, open to new ideas, open to men and women of both parties, open to the critics as well as those who support us. We want to bridge the generation gap. We want to bridge the gap between races. We want to bring America together."[9]

Only time would tell if the newly elected president of the United States could achieve this goal.

7

Mr. President

Among the most pressing problems facing Nixon in the White House was the continuing war in Vietnam. Like Johnson and Kennedy before him, Nixon was opposed to the spread of communism throughout Asia. Nixon had promised the voters that he had a plan to end the war in Vietnam. Now he had to live up to that promise.

On March 16, 1969, Nixon met with Presidential Assistant for National Security Affairs Henry Kissinger, Secretary of State William P. Rogers, and Secretary of Defense Melvin R. Laird. He told them that North Vietnamese Communist troops were using the neighboring country of Cambodia as a base for their operations in Vietnam. The only way to get the Communists to negotiate an honorable end to the war, he said, was "to do something on the military front . . . something they will understand."[1]

The very next day, American planes began bombing Cambodia.

At first, Nixon kept the bombings a secret from the American public. Since Cambodia and the United States were not officially at war, Nixon did not want to admit that he had attacked a neutral country. Cambodia's Prince Norodom Sihanouk actually welcomed the raids. He was eager to have the North Vietnamese chased from his land. If he spoke publicly about the bombings, the public might force Nixon to halt the raids before the job was done.[2]

There was still another reason for Nixon's secrecy—the growing antiwar demonstrations in the United States. If the bombings were made public, hundreds of thousands of Americans already tired of the war would take to the streets in protest. Antiwar protestors were marching in the capitol and throughout the streets of America. Nixon mistakenly believed that by keeping news of the bombings secret, he could win the war that much faster.[3]

But news of the bombings became public when *The New York Times* learned about them and began writing articles detailing the secret war waged in Cambodia. In response, Nixon admitted that United States troops had been sent into Cambodia to seek out and destroy North Vietnamese and Viet Cong supply bases there.

New demonstrations erupted from coast to coast. Nixon was furious with *The New York Times* for releasing the story.[4] Once again, he had come face-to-face with the enemy, and once again, it was the press.

On May 14, 1969, Nixon delivered his first major television address on the subject of Vietnam. He told the nation that he had developed a plan for a negotiated settlement to end the fighting and bring American troops home. He asked all Americans to be patient, saying, "The time has come for new initiatives."[5] A short while later, he announced a program for the gradual withdrawal of a small number of American troops from South Vietnam. The following September, he announced a second troop withdrawal, and in a televised address on November 3, he told the nation about a cooperative United States-South Vietnamese plan to bring all United States troops home and to leave the fighting to the North and South Vietnamese.

One of the purposes of the announcement was to convince the North Vietnamese that the United States was serious about ending the war and wanted to encourage them to come to the peace table. But it was not to be.

After the announcement of troop withdrawals, Ho Chi Minh (hoh chee mihn), the leader of the North

Vietnamese, assembled his advisers to lay out a plan that would carry North Vietnam to victory. The North Vietnamese believed they could outwait the United States for an end to the war. They began sending small bands of guerrilla fighters to attack the enemy in the South. Minh addressed his nation over Radio Hanoi. He warned the North Vietnamese that, despite Nixon's announcement of troop withdrawals, the war in the South was gearing up. The North Vietnamese people, he said, had to "be prepared to fight many years more" until the American enemy "gives up his aggressive design."[6]

As the war in South Vietnam heated up, Nixon decided to attack additional Communist strongholds in Cambodia. On the evening of April 30, 1970, as he addressed the nation about his new Cambodian "incursion," a United States and South Vietnamese force of twenty thousand men, supported by American aircraft, launched an attack against two major North Vietnamese bases in Cambodia.

Instead of finding tens of thousands of Communist soldiers in the camps, the drive netted little more than a new round of criticism from the press. Most of the North Vietnamese, having learned in advance of the coming attack, had fled Cambodia weeks earlier and were hard at work shifting their center of operations to the northernmost provinces of South Vietnam. Despite his promise to the American people that the peace they were seeking was in sight, Nixon had merely succeeded in prolonging the very war he had vowed to end.

Meanwhile, the antiwar movement at home continued to grow. The press lashed out at Nixon daily. A growing number of people felt that the president had lied about having a plan to end the war. Teachers, lawyers, businesspeople, and clergy joined with students throughout the country to protest the bombings.[7] The demonstrations came to a head on May 4, 1970, when protesting students at Kent State University were met by members of Ohio's National Guard. Several guard members fired into the crowd, killing four youths.

The slayings sparked protests across the country. Americans blamed Nixon and his wartime policies for the killings. More than four hundred colleges and universities shut down as students and professors took to the streets. Nearly one hundred thousand demonstrators marched in Washington, demanding Nixon's impeachment.

Meanwhile, Nixon had turned his attention to other nations. In his first year in office, he visited Belgium, England, West Germany, Italy, and France in an effort to strengthen the North Atlantic Treaty Organization (NATO). He took a tour of the Philippines, Indonesia, Thailand, India, Pakistan, and South Vietnam. Then he visited Romania. Nixon was the first American president to travel to a Soviet-bloc nation since World War II. In the fall of 1970, Nixon visited Italy, Spain, Great Britain, and Yugoslavia. He met with NATO commanders, had an audience with Pope Paul VI, and met with political leaders in England and Ireland.

Despite his best efforts, the war in Vietnam continued. Throughout 1971 and 1972, Nixon kept up his efforts to "Vietnamize" the war, to turn it over to the Vietnamese. By the autumn of 1972, United States troop strength in Vietnam, which in April 1969 had reached a peak of 543,000, was down to 32,200.[8]

In early 1972, the North Vietnamese once again mounted an offensive against the South. In an effort to cut off military supply routes to Hanoi, the North Vietnamese capital, Nixon ordered the mining of North Vietnamese ports and the bombing of overland supply routes from China. Nixon attempted to end the war by negotiating with North Vietnam's chief supporters, the People's Republic of China and the Soviet Union. He visited China in February 1972 and the Soviet Union the following May. As a result, the United States and China achieved better relations. The United States and the Soviet Union reached an agreement to limit the manufacture of nuclear weapons. They also decided to pool their resources in space exploration and in medical and environmental research, but they failed to reach an agreement on Vietnam.

In September 1971, President Nixon signed a bill authorizing the extension of the draft and an increase in military pay. The war in Vietnam was a primary concern during his first term as president.

Finally, in October 1972, the United States and North Vietnam agreed to end the fighting. But South Vietnam's government refused to honor the United States-backed agreement. The war raged on. The United States, which had promised to support South Vietnam to the end, was caught between that promise and Nixon's desire to bring the last American troops home.

Nixon needed a plan to ensure his reelection to the presidency. He had already spent more money on his campaign than any other presidential candidate in history. He had used the power of every government agency at his disposal to help ensure his reelection, but it wasn't enough. Nor was it enough to know that the Democrats were in trouble.

That hadn't been the case earlier in the campaign. Then the Democrats had three strong candidates to mount against him. Senator Edward M. "Ted" Kennedy, the youngest brother of the former president of the United States, was the front-runner and certainly someone for Nixon to fear. Senators Edmund Muskie and Hubert Humphrey were also leading candidates for the Democratic primary.

Then, one by one, the candidates began dropping out. The first was Kennedy, who gave as his reason only that he did not want the position, that he thought he should remain in the Senate for four more years.

The next to leave the race was Muskie. He had done poorly in the primary elections in the spring of 1972 and was perceived as a weak-willed candidate with little chance of defeating Nixon.

That left Hubert Humphrey. He worked hard for his party's nomination, but had a poor showing in the California primary. Humphrey, too, withdrew from the race.

George Wallace, the candidate who had run surprisingly well during the 1968 campaign, was still running on the Independent ticket and was a possible threat to Nixon. Wallace had done well in several early primary elections. Then, while visiting a shopping center in Maryland on May 15, he was shot in an attempted assassination and was left paralyzed from the waist down. He, too, withdrew from the race.

The sole survivor was South Dakota governor George McGovern, the weakest of all the Nixon challengers. McGovern was an energetic spokesman for America's antiwar groups. He had once taught history in college and had served briefly in the Kennedy administration before entering the Senate in 1968. He hardly looked the part of a serious presidential candidate. He was intelligent enough and was certainly likeable, but he had little political strength and a limited political following outside his home state.

Still, it was Nixon's old enemy, the press, that may

have killed McGovern's chances even before he got started. Television coverage at the Democratic National Convention in Miami Beach, Florida, showed McGovern winning the presidential nomination on the first vote, which made the Democratic party look united. That was certainly to its advantage. It also showed some of McGovern's most offbeat political supporters: antiwar demonstrators, abortion rights activists, draft-card burners, and even military deserters. Actress Shirley MacLaine described McGovern's supporters as "a couple of high schools, a grape boycott, a Black Panther rally, and four or five politicians who walked in the wrong door."[9] (The Black Panther party was a militant black-rights group that often found itself in trouble with the law.) Throughout the week-long event, the cameras sent a steady stream of electronic images to America. The coverage made the Democratic party look unprofessional and disorganized.

After the convention had ended, Democratic congressman James O'Hara said, "I think we lost the [presidential] election at Miami. . . ."[10]

The Democrats were slowly discrediting themselves in the eyes of the public. Still, Nixon had not found the edge he was looking for.

On October 26, just two weeks before the presidential election, political lightning struck. Henry Kissinger, the president's special envoy to Vietnam, went on national television and announced, "Peace is at hand."[11] The news spread among American voters like wildfire. Everyone was convinced that Nixon was finally about to fulfill his 1968 campaign promise to end the long, grueling, and costly war—everyone, that is, except the antiwar protestors. They had heard rumors like this before, and they had not believed them. Now it would be up to the American people to determine their fate—and that of a divided America.

The voters who turned out for the election overwhelmingly reelected Nixon and Agnew to another term. Nixon's 60.7 percent of the popular vote was the highest a Republican candidate had ever received in a presidential election. He won a total of 520 electoral votes. McGovern pulled in only seventeen. Nixon took the victory at the polls to mean that the voters—the American public—were solidly behind him.

Once again, Nixon had made a serious miscalculation. A chain of events that had already been set into motion was about to blow up in his face.

8

A Case for the United States Government

Nixon started his second term in office on a high note. The nation was once again feeling good about itself. The economy was up, the war was about to end, and the threat of a nuclear confrontation with the Soviet Union seemed less likely than at any time since World War II.

There was a cloud over the Nixon administration, however. It was called Watergate.

In June 1972, several agents hired by the Committee for the Re-election of the President (CRP) had been arrested while breaking into the Democratic National Committee headquarters at the Watergate apartment-office complex in Washington, D.C. They were attempting to steal information that the Republican party might use to its advantage in the 1972 election. They had also placed an illegal wiretap on Democratic party members' phones.

In January 1973, five of the Plumbers (so named because one of their jobs was to keep information about the Republican party from leaking to the public) pleaded guilty to charges of burglary and political espionage in a trial presided over by federal judge John Sirica. G. Gordon Liddy and James McCord, who pleaded innocent, nonetheless were likewise found guilty and were given long prison terms. The former treasurer of the CRP finance committee, Hugh W. Sloan, revealed that $199,000 had been paid to Liddy in 1972. He had no idea what Liddy had done with the money, but he testified that Attorney General John Mitchell and former commerce secretary Maurice H. Stans knew of the payment. Suddenly, the Watergate break-in had been tied to the Nixon administration.

On February 7, the United States Senate voted 70 to 0 to establish a seven-member committee to investigate Watergate. The committee was headed by Senator Sam Ervin, a tough constitutional lawyer and a Democrat from North Carolina. The next day, Earl Silbert, the federal prosecutor in the case, announced that he was going to bring all seven defendants in the case before a grand jury to try to find out just how high up in the White House the Watergate affair had reached.

The Senate committee soon called Nixon's White House counsel, John W. Dean III, to come before it to testify. Dean stalled. If he appeared before the committee, he'd have to tell the truth about what he knew. That could be damaging to the Nixon administration. Stalling was the best tactic.

"Of course," Nixon said, "I am not dumb and I will never forget when I heard about this forced entry [break-in] and bugging. I thought, What [. . .] is this? What is the matter with these people? Are they crazy? I thought they were nuts! A prank! I think our Democratic friends know that, too, [although] they think I have people capable of it. And they are correct, . . ."

Then, after pausing for several moments, Nixon added, "But let's remember this was not done by the White House. This was done by the Committee to Re-elect, and [John] Mitchell was the Chairman. . . . Mitchell won't allow himself to be ruined. He will put on his big stone face."[1]

On March 13, 1972, the Senate Judiciary Committee voted to have Dean testify before the committee on the nomination of Patrick Gray. Gray had been nominated to become the new head of the Federal Bureau of Investigation (FBI). Dean, concerned that he might be asked questions about Watergate, first talked with the president and then declined the invitation. Both he and

On February 7, 1973, the United States Senate voted 70 to 0 to establish a seven-member committee to investigate Watergate. Only time would tell if they would link Nixon to any wrongdoing.

Nixon felt that the committee would not be satisfied with sending the Watergate Plumbers to jail. They wanted the burglars to identify participants higher up in the Nixon administration, and they would use any means they could to accomplish this.[2]

The committee asked White House aide H. R. "Bob" Haldeman to talk. Dean told Nixon that Haldeman didn't know much, but when Nixon asked Dean if Haldeman's assistant, Gordon Strachan, knew about the break-in, Dean answered yes.

"He knew?" Nixon asked.

"Yes."

"About the Watergate?"

"Yes," Dean replied.

The president seemed worried. Strachan worked for Haldeman in the White House. Here at last was the link in the chain that could tie the break-in to the administration.

"I will be damned!" Nixon shouted. "Well that is the problem . . . Strachan."

Then Nixon asked Dean about Liddy, who had already been sentenced for his role in the break-in. Would Liddy plea-bargain and offer to reveal other names for a lesser sentence?

Dean said, "He's a strange man, Mr. President."

"Strange or strong?" Nixon asked.

"Both," Dean replied. "But he's also loyal to our side."[3]

The two were satisfied that they could contain the damage done by the break-in so as to avoid any connection to the White House. But on March 19, 1973, James McCord, a defendant in the Watergate case, wrote a letter to Judge Sirica saying that some of the other defendants had lied in court. He told Sirica that high-up Nixon administration officials, who had not yet been identified in court, were involved in persuading the defendants to remain silent about their knowledge of the incident—to cover it up. He was revealing this information, he said, because he wanted to come clean—and he feared for his life.

On April 31, 1973, on national radio and television, Nixon announced that his two main White House aides, Bob Haldeman and John Ehrlichman, were resigning. So, too, was Attorney General Richard Kleindienst (who had been named to the post after Mitchell had resigned). White House counsel John Dean had been dismissed.

In June, Dean appeared before the committee and testified that Nixon had lied to the nation. Dean insisted that Nixon had known about attempts to cover up the Watergate affair since September 1972, at least. Furthermore, Dean told the committee, Nixon kept an "enemies list" of hundreds of names. The White House regularly harassed these people through illegal tax investigations and other means.[4] This was extraordinary information, but the committee had no way of proving whether or not it was true.

Then, the following month, Alexander Butterfield, a former White House aide, revealed that Nixon had installed voice-activated audiotape recorders so that he could secretly tape all of his White House conversations. Here, at last, was a chance to get to the bottom of Watergate involvement. The committee requested that the White House turn some of the tapes over to them for review. Nixon refused, claiming that he had executive privilege in such matters, meaning that he was exempt from the committee's authority.

The new attorney general, Elliot Richardson, appointed Harvard law professor Archibald Cox as the special prosecutor for the case. Cox subpoenaed the tapes. Nixon refused to release them to him, too. Finally, Cox took the case to court, and Judge Sirica upheld Cox's demand for the release of the tapes. Nixon responded by taking the case to the United States Court of Appeals, which backed Sirica's ruling.

Then, on October 10, 1973, only ten months into his second term, Vice President Agnew was forced to resign. Agnew had been under investigation on charges that he had been involved in political corruption during his years in Maryland politics and afterward. United States attorneys uncovered kickbacks (illegal financial payments) to Agnew made by Baltimore County building contractors while Agnew was county executive of Baltimore, governor of Maryland, and vice president.

Agnew pleaded no contest to a charge of evading federal income tax and was sentenced to three years of probation and fined $10,000. Eventually, he was ordered to repay the state of Maryland more than $248,000 for bribes he took while in state office.[5]

Following Agnew's resignation, the president named Michigan congressman Gerald R. Ford to the position of vice president. Ford was quickly approved by Congress.

Meanwhile, the congressional hearings on Watergate continued. Each day, the Nixon administration became more deeply involved in the controversy. On October 20, Nixon ordered Attorney General Richardson to fire Special Prosecutor Cox because Cox still sought the release of key White House tapes. Richardson refused and resigned. Nixon then ordered Deputy Attorney General William Ruckelshaus to fire Cox. Ruckelshaus also refused and resigned.

Finally, Nixon named Robert Bork, the solicitor general, to the position of acting attorney general, and he, too, was ordered to fire Cox, which he did. The special prosecutor's office was abolished under Nixon's command.

Three days later, after mounting pressure from Congress and the public, Nixon reversed his decision and offered to release typed transcripts of the tapes Cox had requested. He also reestablished the special prosecutor's office and appointed Leon Jaworski to continue the investigation into Watergate. Jaworski rejected the president's offer of the transcripts and continued to pressure Nixon for the original tapes. Instead, on April 30, 1974, Nixon released 1,216 pages of highly edited transcripts concerning the Watergate incident. The transcripts contained suspicious gaps in several conversations.

On May 9, the House Judiciary Committee began its formal hearings on the impeachment of the president. Two weeks later, Jaworski, in a last-ditch effort to obtain the tapes, petitioned the United States Supreme Court to hear the case *United States* v. *Richard M. Nixon.*

On July 8, 1974, the Court heard oral arguments for the United States. Special Prosecutor Jaworski approached the podium and addressed the Justices:

> Mr. Chief Justice, and may it please the Court:
>
> On March 1 last, a United States District Court grand jury, sitting here, returned an indictment against seven defendants charging various offenses, including among them a conspiracy to defraud the United States, and also to obstruct justice. John Mitchell, one of the defendants, was a former attorney general of the United States, and also chairman of the Committee to Re-elect the President. Another, H.R. Haldeman, was the President's chief of staff. Another, John Ehrlichman, was

assistant to the President for domestic affairs. The others were either on the President's staff or held responsible positions on the reelection committee.

In the course of its deliberations, the grand jury voted unanimously, with nineteen members concurring, that the course of events in the formation and continuation of a conspiracy was such that President Nixon, among a number of others, should be identified as an unindicted coconspirator....

Now, although this particular decision and determination on the part of the grand jury occurred in February, it was a well-kept secret for two and a half months. The grand jury, of course, knew it; the members of the prosecution staff knew it. It was done so as to avoid affecting the proceedings in the House Judiciary Committee [which was considering the impeachment of the President]...

Now, on April 30, the President released to the public and submitted to the House Judiciary Committee 1,216 pages [of] edited transcripts of 43 conversations dealing with Watergate—portions of 20 of the subpoenaed conversations were included among the 43. Then on May 1, by his counsel, [he] filed a special appearance, a formal claim of privilege and a motion to quash [to annul or overthrow] the subpoena.[6]

After some additional exchanges between Jaworski and several of the Justices, the special prosecutor made an attempt to provide the Court with an overview of what by now had become a very complicated case.

Now, may I, before I get to the jurisdictional points, briefly state what we consider to be a bird's-eye view of this case. Now enmeshed in almost 500 pages of briefs, when boiled down, this case really presents one fundamental issue: Who is to be the arbiter of what the

Constitution says? Basically, this is not a novel question—although the factual situation involved is, of course, unprecedented. There are corollary questions to be sure. But in the end, after the rounds have been made, we return to face these glaring facts that I want to briefly review for a final answer.

Stewart: Right. He is submitting his position to the Court and asking us to agree with it. He went first to the district court, and he has petitioned in this Court. He has himself invoked the judicial process, and he has submitted to it.

Jaworski: Well, that is not entirely correct, Mr. Justice.

Stewart: Didn't he file a motion to quash the subpoenas in the District Court of the United States?

Jaworski: Sir, he has also taken the position that we have no standing in the court to have this issue heard. . . .

Stewart: As a matter of law, his position is that he is the sole judge, and he is asking this Court to agree with that proposition, as a matter of constitutional law.

Jaworski: What I am saying is that if he is the sole judge, and if he is to be considered the sole judge, and he is in error in his interpretation, then he goes on being in error in his interpretation.

Stewart: Then this Court will tell him so. That is what this case is about, isn't it?

Jaworski: Well, that is what I think the case is about, yes, sir.[7]

After an agreement had been reached about the exact purpose of the hearing, Justice William O. Douglas resumed the questioning.

Douglas: Well, we start with a Constitution that does

not contain the words "executive privilege," is that right?

Jaworski: That is right, sir.

Douglas: So why don't we go on from there?

Jaworski: All right, sir. That is a very good beginning point. But of course there are other things that need to be discussed, inasmuch as they have been raised.

In refusing to produce the evidence sought by a subpoena . . . in the criminal trial of the seven defendants [the five burglars in Watergate, H. R. Haldeman, and John Ehrlichman]—among them former aides and devotees—the President invokes the provisions of the Constitution. His counsel's brief is replete with references to the Constitution as justifying his position. In his public statements, as we all know, the President has embraced the Constitution as offering him support for his refusal to supply the subpoenaed tapes.

Now, the President may be right in how he reads the Constitution. But he may also be wrong. And if he is wrong, who is there to tell him so? If there is no one, then the President, of course, is free to pursue his course of erroneous interpretations. What then becomes of our constitutional form of government? So when counsel for the President in his brief states that this case goes to the heart of our basic constitutional system, we agree. Because in our view, this nation's constitutional form of government is in serious jeopardy if the President, any president, is to say that the Constitution means what he says it does, and that there is no one, not even the Supreme Court, to tell him otherwise.[8]

At this point in the argument, Justice Potter Stewart interrupted Jaworski with a question.

Stewart: Mr. Jaworski, the President went to a court. He went to the district court with this motion to quash, and then he filed a cross petition here. He is asking the Court to say that his position is correct as a matter of law, is he not?

Jaworski: He is saying his position is correct because he interprets the Constitution that way.

[Justice Warren E.] Burger: Perhaps we can further narrow the area if, as I take it from your brief, you do emphasize there is no claim here of typical military secrets, or diplomatic secrets, or what in the Burr case [*United States* v. *Burr*, 1807] were referred to as State secrets. None of those things are in this case; is that right?

Jaworski: That is correct, sir. . . . I think that we realize that there is at stake the matter of the supplying of evidence that relates to two former close aides and devotees. I think we are aware of the fact that the President has publicly stated that he believed that these two aides of his, Mr. Haldeman and Mr. Ehrlichman, would come out all right in the end. Added to that the fact that the President has a sensitivity of his own involvement is also a matter that calls for the exercise of the question to which Mr. Justice Douglas alluded as one that is somewhat unusual. . . .[9]

The Court determined that it had jurisdiction in the case—that is, it had a right and an obligation to hear the case, rather than to send it back to a lower court for additional review. That determination was followed by a clarification of Jaworski's role as special prosecutor in the case. Finally, Jaworski continued his argument by saying that there is nothing in the Constitution that relates to the right of the president to exercise executive privilege.

[Justice William J.] Brennan: Is the term "executive privilege" an ancient one?

Jaworski: I beg your pardon, sir?

Brennan: Is the term "executive privilege" an ancient one?

Jaworski: It has been used over a period of time. How ancient, Mr. Justice Brennan, I am not in a position to say. But certainly it has been one that has been used over the years. But it is not one that I find any basis for in the Constitution.

Stewart: Are you now arguing that there is no such thing as executive privilege?

Jaworski: No, sir.

Stewart: I didn't think so.

Jaworski: No, sir. Because I say there is no basis for it in the Constitution.

Stewart: You think if anything it's a common-law privilege? Is that your point?

Jaworski: Yes, sir. It has been traditionally recognized and appropriately so in a number of cases as we see it. We do not think it is an appropriate one in this case. But we certainly do not for a moment feel that it has any constitutional base.

Burger: In Scheuer against Rhodes I thought we held that there is a common-law privilege in the executives dealing at the state level, but that it is a qualified privilege, is that not so?

Jaworski: Yes, Mr. Chief Justice, that is exactly the

point. This Court has examined a number of situations [involving executive privilege]. In some situations, as I think was pointed out earlier, where military secrets and such as that were involved, or national secrets of great importance, the Court has taken a good, close look, and has upheld privilege.[10]

Jaworski emphasized his beliefs that this case involved the specific refusal of the President to turn over tape recordings that he claimed were protected under executive privilege. Yet there appeared to be no precedent for such protection in law.

> **Jaworski:** On the issue of executive privilege, I should point out here it is a very narrow one. I think it is important that we bear this in mind. . . .
>
> We know that there are sovereign prerogatives to protect the confidentiality necessary to carry out responsibilities in the fields of international relations and national defense that are not here involved. There is no claim of any State secrets, or that disclosure will have dire effects on the nation or its people. . . .[11]

This is a summary of Jaworski's three questions to the Supreme Court:

1. Does the Supreme Court have jurisdiction over the case?
2. Does the Court have the authority to decide whether or not executive privilege exists within the law, even though it is never mentioned in the United States Constitution?
3. If the Court decides that the principle of executive privilege exists within the law, under what circumstances may the president apply it?

9

A Case for
Richard M. Nixon

Following Leon Jaworski's opening arguments, James D. St. Clair gave his opening statement on behalf of Nixon. St. Clair argued that the real case before the Court was not the question of executive privilege. The question was whether or not the Court should hear the case at all.

If the Court heard the case and decided on it, St. Clair argued, it would influence the House Judiciary Committee's hearings on the impeachment of the president. When Justice Douglas commented that the sole authority to impeach is in the House and not in the courts, St. Clair agreed. Justice Thurgood Marshall asked why, then, St. Clair thought that the Supreme Court's hearing of the case would be improper. It soon became clear that St. Clair was in trouble from the start.

>**Douglas:** . . .This case should be dismissed as improvidently [mistakenly] granted, shouldn't it?

>**St. Clair:** Exactly right, sir. Not only that, it makes the case unjusticiable [unable to be decided by the Court], at least.

>**Marshall:** Then the district court's decision [that Nixon should turn over the tapes to the special prosecutor] stands. Is that what you want?

>**St. Clair:** No. The case should be dismissed, sir.

>**Marshall:** If we dismiss [the case] as improvidently granted, I submit that the district court's judgment would stand.

>**St. Clair:** Then I would retract what I said. . . .

>**Stewart:** The case would be on appeal in the court of appeals.

At this point, Chief Justice Burger joined the argument, trying to gain insight into exactly what it was that the president's counsel hoped to achieve.

>**Burger:** Are you now talking about the bypassing of the court of appeals?

>**St. Clair:** No, sir. I am talking about the proceeding before the district court, through the court of appeals, to this Court.

>**Burger:** If we dismissed this appeal as improvidently granted, it would go back to the court of appeals.

>**St. Clair:** Well, as I say, I think this case should be dismissed—period.

83

Burger: No. Really what you mean is you think that the order of Judge Sirica should be vacated and set aside.

St. Clair: That is right, sir.

Brennan: That is quite different from dismissing the case.

St. Clair: I agree.

Douglas: That's deciding it on the merits.

St. Clair: That's right. That is what I am trying to get across to this Court, perhaps unartfully—this case should be disposed of, be it by vacating the order below or not. In any event, it is improper in our view that this case should be heard in the context it is now being heard. We wouldn't be here, on July 8, before a crowded courtroom, if it was not recognized generally. . . .

Douglas: It is a political question here, and it was a political question in the district court.

St. Clair: Exactly. Therefore it is a nonjusticiable issue in this and in the district court.[1]

St. Clair then went on to emphasize his belief that the Court should not decide the case before them because the House committee was presently arguing the subject of whether or not to impeach the president. Once again, he found himself in trouble.

Marshall: What in those tapes involves the impeachment proceedings?

St. Clair: Pardon?

Marshall: What in any of these tapes is involved in the impeachment proceeding?

St. Clair: Well, if your Honor please, the House of Representatives has subpoenaed—

Marshall: I don't know what is in the tapes. I assume you do.

St. Clair: No, I don't.

Marshall: You don't know, either? Well, how do you know that they are subject to executive privilege?

St. Clair: Well, I do know that there is a preliminary showing that they are conversations between the President and his close aides.

Marshall: Regardless of what it is?

St. Clair: Regardless of what it is. They may involve a number of subjects.

Marshall: But you don't know.

Burger: Does not the special prosecutor claim that the subject matter is the same [relating to Watergate]?

St. Clair: He claims that, but he has no way of showing it. In fact, he says it is only probable or likely. He has no way of showing that they in fact involve the subject of Watergate.

Douglas: If his claim is honored by the Court, all that would happen is the evidence would go to Judge Sirica, who would examine it in camera [in privacy], I assume.

St. Clair: I presume that is so. It would then be made available to the special prosecutor. The special prosecutor says this of course would then become part of the impeachment proceedings, and there we are.[2]

After a brief additional exchange, Justice Marshall came up with a question that had not previously been asked by the Court.

>Marshall: Why were you [the President] willing to give up twenty-some of them [the tapes]?

>St. Clair: That is a very good question, and I would like to answer it. The decisions that are made in the impeachment proceedings, Justice Marshall, are essentially political decisions.

>Marshall: I'm talking about this case. You say he will give up twenty of them in this case.

>St. Clair: Yes, we will, because they have already been made public.

>Marshall: The tapes, or transcriptions?

>St. Clair: As soon as the judge approves some method of validating the accuracy of these tapes, they can have the tapes. But you have to understand, the tape is a part of a reel. A reel may cover a dozen conversations. So there is a mechanical problem of trying to validate or be sure that this is correct. But it is only a mechanical problem. Once that is solved, subject to the approval of the judge below [Judge Sirica], they have the availability of that.

>Marshall: Are the tapes that you are willing to release valuable to the Watergate committee in Congress?

>St. Clair: We think so. That is why we made them available.

>Marshall: I thought you said you didn't want them to have any tapes.

>St. Clair: No, sir.

Throughout Nixon's political career—both the ups and downs—his wife Pat remained by his side. Here, they are standing with their two daughters and their husbands.

Marshall: That this was merely a way of getting stuff over to them. But you are going to give them some.

St. Clair: I say this: I say the President should decide as a political matter what should be made available to the House.

Marshall: Oh.

St. Clair: That the Court ought not to be drawn into that decision.

Marshall: And that's final. Nobody can do anything about it.

St. Clair: The House takes a different view. The House has subpoenaed something in the neighborhood of 145 tapes, and that is a political decision.

Marshall: So that the House can get them, the President can get them, and the only people I know that cannot get them is the courts.

St. Clair: The President has not honored any of the subpoenas other than the first one issued by the House. So that there is a dispute in the House now between the President and the Committee on the Judiciary. It is essentially a political dispute. It is a dispute that this Court ought not be drawn into. And the result of a decision in this case would . . . result in [this Court's] being brought into it.

Brennan: You have not convinced me that we are drawn into it by deciding this case. How are we drawn into the impeachment proceedings by deciding this case?

St. Clair: The impact of a decision in this case undeniably, Mr. Justice Brennan, in my view, cannot have—will not be overlooked [by the House Judiciary Committee].[3]

Justice Douglas asked St. Clair if the good done by releasing the tapes wasn't better than the possibility that the tapes might somehow affect the outcome of the House's impeachment hearings.

> **Douglas:** . . . The beneficiaries here are six defendants [Watergate burglars] being tried for criminal charges. What the President has may free them completely. Is that true? Theoretically . . .
>
> **St. Clair:** Mr. Justice Douglas—it may . . . What is before this Court is a prosecutor's [Jaworski's] demand for evidence. I direct my remarks for a moment to that problem. He says that in effect we have no right to be here. . . . But even he contends that we did not delegate to him what presidential conversations would be used as evidence. . . . And that is what is at issue there. Not when and who is to be indicted, but what Presidential communications are going to be used as evidence. That is what the issue is in this case.[4]

After a long debate on the constitutionality of releasing the tapes, Justice Powell asked St. Clair if he would withhold the tapes from release even if they concerned a criminal act. St. Clair said he would, because executive privilege is the same regardless of the subject of the tapes. At that point, the Court asked St. Clair if he would feel the same way even if the tape were of a conversation between a hypothetical president who was illegally paying off a judge with money.

> **St. Clair:** I would think that that could not be released, if it were a confidential communication. If the

President did appoint such an individual the remedy is clear—the remedy is he [the President] should be impeached. . . .

Marshall: How are you going to impeach him if you don't know about it?

St. Clair: Well, if you know about it, then you can state the case. If you don't know about it, you don't have it.

Marshall: So there you are. You're on the prongs of a dilemma, huh?

St. Clair: No, I don't think so.

Marshall: If you know the President is doing something wrong, you can impeach him. But the only way you can find out is this way [by reviewing the tapes; but you can't review the tapes, so] you can't impeach him, so you don't impeach him. You lose me someplace along there.

St. Clair: . . . Human experience has not demonstrated that's a fact; very few things forever are hidden. Secondly, however, this case is not that case. As I point out, there is a plethora of information [about the Watergate break-in]. This is not a case where there is no information. If anything, there is more than enough.[5]

St. Clair had tried to raise five major questions:

1. Should the Supreme Court hear the case currently before it?
2. Was this case a political matter, in which case the Court should not hear it, or a constitutional matter, in which case the Court would hear it?
3. If the case was a political matter, shouldn't the Court vacate, or reverse, the lower court's ruling that the president release the tapes?

4. Should the Court refuse to hear the case because doing so might influence the House Judiciary Committee's impeachment hearings?

5. Does the president have a right to executive privilege regarding any private conversations, no matter what the subject matter?

Finally, the Court next heard a closing argument from Philip A. Lacovara, presenting several additional arguments for the United States against Nixon.

It had been a short, pointed hearing in which the Court was basically left to ponder this question: Does the president have a right to exercise executive privilege whenever he wants to? While the answer might be as simple as "yes" or "no," the consequences of that answer could alter the very future of America. If the Court decided that the president had an unrestricted right to executive privilege, future presidents might claim executive privilege for any one of a number of reasons, not only for the security or defense of the nation. That could turn the president of the United States into something resembling more a tyrant than a democratic representative of the government.

If the Court decided that the president had a restricted right to executive privilege, under what circumstances would those restrictions apply?

10

The Decision

On July 24, 1974, Chief Justice Warren Burger read the unanimous decision of the Court. In an 8–0 verdict, with Justice William H. Rehnquist not participating, the Court found that the president *was* entitled to greater than normal rights, especially in matters of national defense and security. In the case of *United States* v. *Nixon,* however, the special prosecutor had asked for specific tapes that had *no bearing* on national defense or security. His request for the tapes was based upon a specific need to determine which of the Watergate defendants were innocent and which were guilty. Furthermore, Nixon's claim that the tapes were confidential had already been weakened by the fact that he had already released the contents of some of the subpoenaed tapes.

Burger said that the general claims of the president for the need to be above the law did not stand up to the specific claims of the justice system when it came to prosecuting a criminal case such as Watergate.[1]

The Court was careful to retain the notion that the president has certain privileges and immunities that other Americans do not have, most notably in matters of national defense and security. It went to great pains, however, to point out that such privileges are conditional, depending upon individual circumstances, and that those circumstances *did not exist* in this case.

In the end, the Court ordered the tapes released to the special prosecutor. This was a devastating blow to Nixon. As it turned out, the tapes contained the smoking gun—the unmistakable proof—that linked the president to a conspiracy to obstruct justice. After the tapes had been released, Nixon, trying to sidestep the damage done to himself and to his administration, admitted publicly that the evidence held within the tapes was "at variance" with earlier statements he had made and agreed that he would "respect and accept the court's decision."[2]

Nixon contemplated his next move. He had been caught in the act of trying to cover up the Watergate affair. He had been caught lying. Perhaps the release of future tapes would reveal even greater involvement, even more guilt. Now the question remaining for him was where to go from there; what should he do next? That was about to be answered for him.

On July 27, 1974, the House Judiciary Committee voted 27–11 to recommend to the full House that the president be impeached for criminal acts committed while in office. The decision was based upon three counts: obstruction of justice, abuse of presidential powers, and trying to stop the impeachment process by ignoring the committee's subpoenas. The Articles of Impeachment read in part: "Richard Nixon has acted in a manner contrary to his trust as President and subversive of Constitutional government, to the great prejudice of law and justice and to the manifest injury of the people of the U.S."[3]

On August 5, Nixon reluctantly released three tapes to the public. One of them concerned a talk he had had with H. R. Haldeman on June 23, 1972. Nixon had insisted that he knew nothing of the Watergate break-in that had occurred only six days prior, but the tape revealed Nixon talking with Haldeman about former Attorney General John Mitchell's involvement in the burglary, Nixon ordering a cover-up of the break-in, and Nixon's plan to use the FBI and CIA to protect himself. It also included obscene comments made against Jews, women, homosexuals, Italians, and the press.[4]

Public reaction to the tapes was overwhelmingly negative. Even fellow conservative Republicans and longtime Nixon supporters Ronald Reagan, Barry Goldwater, and George Bush demanded the president's resignation. Still, Nixon was not prepared to give up.

Faced with being impeached by the House, Nixon called for an aide to count the number of senators known to be in support of impeachment. He needed at least thirty-four not-guilty votes in the Senate to prevent him from being convicted. The aide told him he would get only seven.

The reality of the situation may have been even worse. Public support for Nixon in Congress had all but disappeared. Of the 435 members of the House, only two had come out publicly against impeachment. Of the one hundred members of the Senate, only one had rushed to Nixon's defense.

Nixon called his secretary, Rosemary Woods, into his office. He told her to inform his family that "the whole bunch is deserting now and we have no way to lobby them or keep them."[5] Then he pulled out a pad and began jotting down notes for the most important speech of his life. He was preparing to resign.

He called his press secretary, Ron Ziegler, and Chief of Staff Alexander Haig into his office and told them he would make his resignation speech on the evening of

August 8. "I will do it with no rancor and no loss of dignity. I will do it gracefully."

They stared silently at the president. Finally Nixon added, "Well, I [messed] it up good, real good, didn't I?"[6]

At 9:01 P.M. on August 8, 1974, Richard Nixon faced the television cameras from his Oval Office desk for the last time. He spoke in general about having lost the support of Congress and having suffered personal agony during the preceding months. He announced calmly and with little apparent emotion: "I have never been a quitter. To leave office before my term is completed is abhorrent to every instinct in my body. But as President I must put the interests of America first. . . . Therefore, I shall resign the presidency effective at noon tomorrow."[7]

He went on to thank his supporters and reviewed some of the achievements of his administration. He said he was confident that "the world is a safer place today . . . and that all of our children have a better chance than before of living in peace rather than dying in war" because of his efforts.[8]

Finally, he ended his speech with a prayer: "May God's grace be with you in all the days ahead."[9]

There was still a chance that Nixon might be prosecuted, even though he was no longer in office. But, Gerald Ford, who had assumed the presidency when

Richard M. Nixon packed up his belongings in the Oval Office before he gave his resignation speech on August 8, 1972.

Nixon resigned, issued a presidential pardon excusing Nixon for any crimes he had committed in connection with Watergate.

Richard M. Nixon was the only president ever forced to resign from office under the threat of impeachment. He had been found guilty of obstruction of justice. He had lost the support of nearly everyone near and dear to him—except his family, who stood behind him both publicly and privately for the rest of his life.

He died on April 22, 1994, at the age of eighty-one. Will future generations remember him for his long years of political service and his contributions to national affairs? He did, after all, cut military spending, tie Social Security benefits to increases in the cost of living, and lower the voting age to eighteen. Will they remember him for his postpresidential role as unofficial United States ambassador and for his contributions to international politics? Certainly all these things go into the record of Richard Nixon's presidency. More than anything else, though, he will be recalled for his role in Watergate.

If anything positive came out of one of the most tragic eras in American political history, it was the finding of the United States Supreme Court on that day in July 1974. *United States* v. *Nixon* settled once and for all just how much individual power the president of the United States has while in office.

Appendix:
Watergate Events

1971	June 13	President Nixon authorized establishing a "special investigations unit to stop security leaks and to investigate other sensitive matters." The unit became known as the Plumbers.
	August 16	John Dean, White House counsel, prepared a memo entitled "Dealing with our Political Enemies." In it he suggested several different ways "we can use the available federal machinery to [deal with] our political enemies." An "enemies list" was drawn up by White House aides and given to President Nixon.
	September	Donald Segretti was hired by the Committee for the Re-election of the President (CRP) to upset the Democratic presidential campaign.
	September 3	The Plumbers broke into the office of psychiatrist Daniel Ellsberg, an outspoken critic of the war in Vietnam. The Central Intelligence Agency (CIA) assisted the leader of the group, ex-agent E. Howard Hunt, by supplying him with a camera, a wig, and a speech-altering device.

1972	April 10	Robert Vesco gave $200,000 in cash to CRP fund-raiser Maurice Stans.
	June 17	Five men were caught breaking into the Democratic National Committee's headquarters in the Watergate building.
	October 10	*Washington Post* reporters Carl Bernstein and Bob Woodward uncovered a CRP plan to upset the 1972 Democratic campaign.
1973	March 19	James McCord, one of the defendants in the Watergate case, sent a letter to Judge John Sirica, claiming that other defendants had committed perjury (lied) and that high White House officials were involved in the Watergate break-in.
	March 21	President Nixon ordered $75,000 to be paid to Watergate defendant E. Howard Hunt in order to keep him quiet.
	April 12	Jeb Magruder, CRP deputy director, admitted that he had committed perjury while testifying about Watergate.
	April 30	H. R. "Bob" Haldeman and John D. Ehrlichman, the two top White House aides, resigned. White House counsel John Dean was dismissed.
	May 16	National television coverage of the Watergate Committee hearings, led by Senator Sam Ervin of North Carolina (D), began.

1973	July 16	White House aide Alexander Butterfield revealed to the Watergate committee that President Nixon had been secretly tape-recording different White House conversations.
	October 20	President Nixon ordered Special Prosecutor Archibald Cox fired. Attorney General Elliott Richardson and Deputy Attorney General William Ruckelshaus both refused and resigned as a result. Acting Attorney General Robert Bork finally fired Cox in what became known as the Saturday Night Massacre.
	November 17	In one of his most famous comments, President Nixon declared in a press conference, "I am not a crook."
1974	April 30	President Nixon released 1,216 pages of highly edited transcripts of several White House tapes.
	May 9	The House Judiciary Committee began official hearings on the impeachment of Nixon.
	July 24	The United States Supreme Court ruled in a unanimous decision that President Nixon had to release sixty-four tapes requested by Special Prosecutor Leon Jaworski.
	July 27	The House Judiciary Committee voted 27–11 to recommend to the full House that President Nixon be impeached.

1974	August 5	President Nixon released transcripts of three tapes that showed he had been involved in a cover-up of the Watergate break-in from six days after the burglary had occurred.
	August 8	President Nixon announced his resignation as president of the United States.
	September 8	President Gerald R. Ford granted Richard M. Nixon a full pardon for his involvement in Watergate.
1975	January 1	A jury found four former Nixon administration officials guilty of crimes concerning Watergate. The four were H. R. Haldeman, John D. Ehrlichman, John N. Mitchell, and Robert C. Mardian.

Chapter Notes

Chapter 1

1. Fred Emery, *Watergate: The Corruption of American Politics and the Fall of Richard Nixon* (New York: Random House, 1994), pp. 269–270.

Chapter 2

1. *Compton's Interactive Encyclopedia,* 1994 (New York: Compton's NewMedia, Inc., 1994).

2. David Wallechinsky and Irving Wallace, eds., *The People's Almanac* (Garden City, N.Y.: Doubleday & Company, 1975), p. 333.

Chapter 3

1. Eric Foner and John A. Garraty, eds., *The Reader's Companion to American History* (Boston: Houghton Mifflin Company, 1991), p. 794.

2. *Compton's Interactive Encyclopedia,* 1994 (New York: Compton's NewMedia, Inc., 1994).

3. Richard Nixon, *In the Arena: A Memoir of Victory, Defeat, and Renewal* (New York: Simon and Schuster, 1990), p. 186; *Los Angeles Mirror,* July 14, 1952, p. 3.

4. Gary Allen, *Richard Nixon: The Man Behind the Mask* (Boston: Western Islands, 1971), p. 129.

5. David Wallechinsky and Irving Wallace, eds., *The People's Almanac* (Garden City, N.Y.: Doubleday & Company, 1975), p. 318.

6. *Compton's Interactive Encyclopedia.*

7. Wallechinsky and Wallace, p. 318.

8. *Compton's Interactive Encyclopedia.*

9. Wallechinsky and Wallace, p. 318.

10. Ibid.

11. Ibid.

Chapter 4

1. Richard Nixon, *In the Arena: A Memoir of Victory, Defeat, and Renewal* (New York: Simon and Schuster, 1990), p. 194.

2. Gary Wills, *Nixon Agonistes* (Boston: Houghton Mifflin Company, 1970), p. 86.

3. David Wallechinsky and Irving Wallace, eds., *The People's Almanac* (Garden City, N.Y.: Doubleday & Company, 1975), p. 319.

4. Gary Allen, *Richard Nixon: The Man Behind the Mask* (Boston: Western Islands, 1971), p. 156.

5. David Halberstam, *The Best and the Brightest* (New York: Random House, 1972), p. 12.

6. Wallechinsky and Wallace, p. 319.

7. Allen, pp. 157–159.

8. Paul F. Boller, Jr., *Presidential Campaigns* (New York: Oxford University Press, 1984), p. 284.

9. *Compton's Interactive Encyclopedia,* 1994 (New York: Compton's NewMedia, Inc., 1994).

10. Boller, p. 284.

11. George S. Hilton, *The Funny Side of Politics* (New York, 1989), p. 236.

12. Peter Lyon, *Eisenhower: Portrait of the Hero* (Boston: Houghton Mifflin Company, 1974), pp. 399–400; David

Halberstam, *The Fifties* (New York: Villard Books, 1993), pp. 127–128.

13. Richard M. Nixon, *Six Crises* (New York: Doubleday and Company, 1962), p. 319.

14. J. Leonard Reinsch, *Getting Elected: From Radio and Roosevelt to Television and Reagan* (New York: Hippocrene Books, 1988), p. 136.

Chapter 5

1. Paul F. Boller, Jr., *Presidential Campaigns* (New York: Oxford University Press, 1984), p. 296.

2. Stefan Lorant, *The Glorious Burden: The American Presidency* (Lenox, Mass.: Authors Edition, 1976), pp. 830, 837.

3. J. Leonard Reinsch, *Getting Elected: From Radio and Roosevelt to Television and Reagan* (New York: Hippocrene Books, 1988), p. 143.

4. Arthur M. Schlesinger, Jr., *A Thousand Days: John F. Kennedy in the White House* (Boston: Houghton Mifflin, 1965), p. 57.

Chapter 6

1. David Wallechinsky and Irving Wallace, eds., *The People's Almanac* (Garden City, N.Y.: Doubleday & Company, 1975), p. 322.

2. Gary Allen, *Richard Nixon: The Man Behind the Mask* (Boston: Western Islands, 1971), p. 217.

3. Ibid., pp. 217–219.

4. Richard M. Nixon, televised concession speech, November 6, 1962.

5. Richard Nixon, *In the Arena: A Memoir of Victory,*

Defeat, and Renewal (New York: Simon and Schuster, 1990), pp. 28–29.

6. "Daley City Under Seige," *Time,* August 30, 1968, p. 18.

7. "The Battle of Chicago," *Newsweek,* September 9, 1968, p. 38.

8. "A Chance to Lead," *Time,* August 16, 1968, p. 10.

9. Ibid.

Chapter 7

1. Stanley Karnow, *Vietnam: A History* (New York: Viking, 1991), p. 606.

2. Ibid., pp. 607–612.

3. Ibid., p. 607.

4. James Reston, *Deadline: A Memoir* (New York: Random House, 1991), pp. 408–409.

5. *Funk and Wagnalls Standard Reference Enclyclopedia Yearbook 1969* (New York: Funk and Wagnalls, 1969), p. 371.

6. Ibid., p. 533.

7. Reston, pp. 352–353.

8. *The 1987 Information Please Almanac* (Boston: Houghton Mifflin Company, 1987), p. 306.

9. Eugene Roseboom and Alfred E. Eckes, Jr., *A History of Presidential Elections* (New York: Macmillan, 1979), p. 297.

10. Ibid., p. 307.

11. Henry Kissinger, nationally televised speech, October 26, 1968.

Chapter 8

1. Stephen E. Ambrose, *Nixon: Ruin and Recovery 1973-1990* (New York: Simon & Schuster, 1991), pp. 70–71.

2. Ibid., p. 71.

3. Ibid., p. 75.

4. Fred Emery, *Watergate: The Corruption of American Politics and the Fall of Richard Nixon* (New York: Random House, 1994), pp. 363–364.

5. *The 1987 Information Please Almanac* (Boston: Houghton Mifflin Company, 1987), p. 126; David Wallechinsky and Irving Wallace, *The People's Almanac #2* (New York: Bantam Books, 1978), p. 478.

6. Oral Arguments to the Supreme Court, *United States v. Richard M. Nixon* and *Richard M. Nixon v. United States*, pp. 839–840.

7. Ibid., pp. 840–841.

8. Ibid., pp. 843–845.

9. Ibid., pp. 845–846.

10. Ibid., pp. 855–856.

11. Ibid., p. 857.

Chapter 9

1. Oral Arguments to the Supreme Court, *United States v. Richard M. Nixon* and *Richard M. Nixon v. United States*, pp. 862–863.

2. Ibid., p. 866.

3. Ibid., pp. 867–868.

4. Ibid., p. 869.

5. Ibid., p. 898.

Chapter 10

1. Leon Jaworski, *The Right and the Power* (New York:

Reader's Digest Press, 1976; Houston: Gulf Publishing Company, 1976), pp. 199–200.

2. Fred Emery, *Watergate: The Corruption of American Politics and the Fall of Richard Nixon* (New York: Random House, 1994), p. 448.

3. Ibid., pp. 443–454.

4. Stephen E. Ambrose, *Nixon: Ruin and Recovery 1973-1990* (New York: Simon & Schuster, 1991), pp. 412–416.

5. Ibid., p. 420.

6. Ibid.

7. Public Papers of the President (Washington, D.C.: Government Printing Office, 1974), pp. 626–629.

8. Ibid.

9. Ibid.

Glossary

argument—A course of reasoning used in court cases. It is intended to persuade others to believe the same way.

civil rights—Equal rights given to persons by laws enacted by civilized communities.

congressman/congresswoman—A member of either the United States House of Representatives or the United States Senate.

decision—A final determination found by a court after an agreed upon consideration or course of action.

dissenting opinion—An opinion that disagrees with the disposition made of a case by the court.

espionage—The act of spying.

executive privilege—The right of the president to withhold information.

federal laws—Laws passed by the United States Congress.

hearing—A proceeding where evidence is taken in order to determine facts and reach a decision on the basis of that evidence.

impeachment—A formal hearing charging a public officer with wrongdoing and removing him or her from office.

indictment—A formal written accusation, drawn up and submitted to a grand jury by a prosecuting attorney, charging someone with a crime.

integration—Mixing people of different races.

judgment—The final determination of the rights of the parties in a lawsuit.

legislator—A member of the United States House of Representatives or the United States Senate.

majority opinion—An opinion that is joined by a majority of the court.

minority opinion—An opinion that is joined by a minority of the court.

opinion—The reason given for a court's judgment, finding, or conclusion.

perjury—Making false statements while under oath.

plaintiff—The person who initially brings suit.

respondent—The person who defends against suit.

segregation—The separation of some people from others, often on the basis of race.

senator—A member of the United States Senate.

Further Reading

Ambrose, Stephen E. *Nixon: Ruin and Recovery, 1973-1990.* New York: Simon & Schuster, 1991.

Bernstein, Carl, and Bob Woodward. *All the President's Men.* New York: Easton, 1974.

———. *The Final Days.* New York: Simon & Schuster, 1976.

Hargrove, Jim. *Richard M. Nixon: 37th President.* Chicago: Children's Press, 1985.

Kane, J. N. *Facts about the Presidents: A Compilation of Biographical and Historical Information,* 5th ed. New York: H. W. Wilson, 1990.

Nixon, R. M. *In the Arena: A Memoir of Victory, Defeat, and Renewal.* New York: Simon & Schuster, 1990.

———. *The Memoirs of Richard Nixon.* New York: Simon & Schuster, 1990.

Index